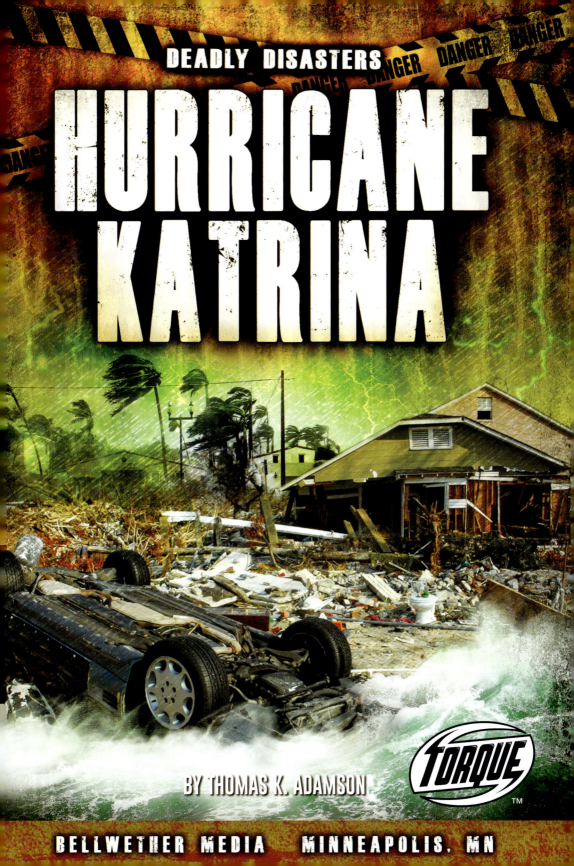

Torque brims with excitement perfect for thrill-seekers of all kinds. Discover daring survival skills, explore uncharted worlds, and marvel at mighty engines and extreme sports. In *Torque* books, anything can happen. Are you ready?

This edition first published in 2022 by Bellwether Media, Inc.

No part of this publication may be reproduced in whole or in part without written permission of the publisher. For information regarding permission, write to Bellwether Media, Inc., Attention: Permissions Department, 6012 Blue Circle Drive, Minnetonka, MN 55343.

Library of Congress Cataloging-in-Publication Data

Names: Adamson, Thomas K., 1970- author.
Title: Hurricane Katrina / by Thomas K. Adamson.
Description: Minneapolis, MN : Bellwether Media, 2022. | Series: Deadly disasters | Includes bibliographical references and index. | Audience: Ages 7-12 | Audience: Grades 4-6 | Summary: "Amazing photography accompanies engaging information about Hurricane Katrina. The combination of high-interest subject matter and light text is intended for students in grades 3 through 7"– Provided by publisher.
Identifiers: LCCN 2021020926 (print) | LCCN 2021020927 (ebook) | ISBN 9781644875292 (library binding) | ISBN 9781648344374 (ebook)
Subjects: LCSH: Hurricane Katrina, 2005–Juvenile literature. | Hurricanes–Gulf States–Juvenile literature. | Hurricanes–Louisiana–Juvenile literature.
Classification: LCC HV636 2005 .U6 A33 2022 (print) | LCC HV636 2005 .U6 (ebook) | DDC 363.34/9220976090511–dc23
LC record available at https://lccn.loc.gov/2021020926
LC ebook record available at https://lccn.loc.gov/2021020927

Text copyright © 2022 by Bellwether Media, Inc. TORQUE and associated logos are trademarks and/or registered trademarks of Bellwether Media, Inc.

Editor: Kieran Downs   Designer: Josh Brink

Printed in the United States of America, North Mankato, MN.

TABLE OF CONTENTS

ROOFTOP RESCUE	4
SUPERSIZED STORM	6
A CITY FLOODS	12
MORE HELP ARRIVES	18
SLOW REBUILD	20
GLOSSARY	22
TO LEARN MORE	23
INDEX	24

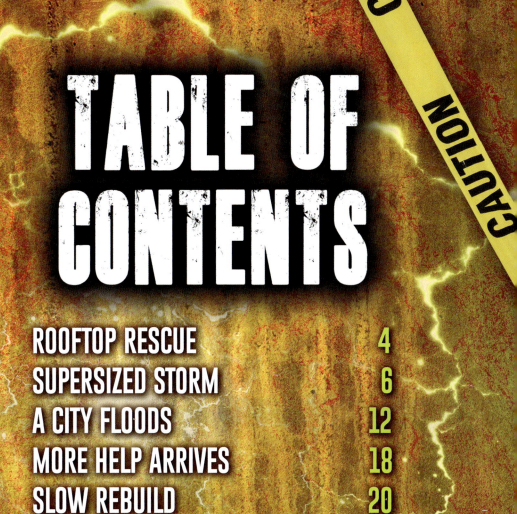

ROOFTOP RESCUE

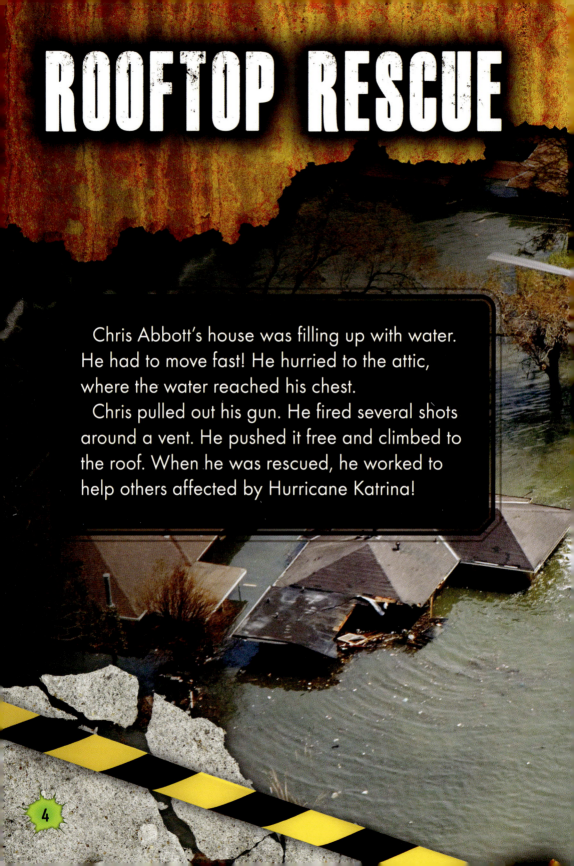

Chris Abbott's house was filling up with water. He had to move fast! He hurried to the attic, where the water reached his chest.

Chris pulled out his gun. He fired several shots around a vent. He pushed it free and climbed to the roof. When he was rescued, he worked to help others affected by Hurricane Katrina!

SUPERSIZED STORM

HURRICANE KATRINA

Hurricanes are powerful storms with strong winds. Hurricane Katrina was one of the strongest hurricanes to ever hit the United States.

Hurricane Katrina formed over the Bahamas on August 23, 2005. It started as a **tropical depression**, but it quickly grew stronger. The next day, it was named a **tropical storm**. It crossed Florida as a Category 1 hurricane.

HOW A HURRICANE BEGINS

SPINNING CLOUDS

COLD AIR = ➡   WARM AIR = ➡

1. AIR RISES FROM WARM OCEAN WATER TO FORM CLOUDS
2. COLD AIR RISES AND WARMS, FORMING MORE CLOUDS
3. WIND CAUSES THE CLOUDS TO SPIN
4. THE STORM GETS STRONGER AS IT CROSSES MORE WARM OCEAN WATER

Katrina gained more strength once it reached the warm waters of the Gulf of Mexico. It became a Category 5 storm on August 28. The storm then turned north and headed for New Orleans, Louisiana.

Much of New Orleans is below sea level. The city often floods when waters rise. But people believed it could handle the storm.

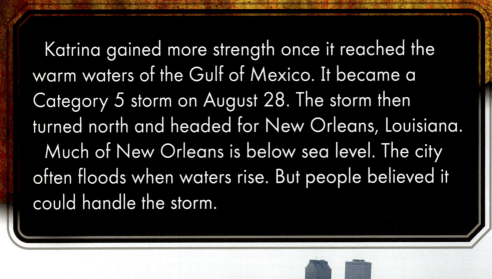

NEW ORLEANS, LOUISIANA

WARNING

On August 28, the National Weather Service issued a clear warning. It said that people would not be able to live in New Orleans for weeks after the storm hit.

SAFFIR-SIMPSON SCALE

CATEGORY 1
wind speeds of 74-95 miles per hour
(119-153 kilometers per hour)

CATEGORY 2
wind speeds of 96-110 miles per hour
(154-177 kilometers per hour)

CATEGORY 3
wind speeds of 111-129 miles per hour
(178-208 kilometers per hour)

CATEGORY 4
wind speeds of 130-156 miles per hour
(209-251 kilometers per hour)

CATEGORY 5
wind speeds of more than 156 miles
(251 kilometers) per hour

People only had a few days to decide what to do. More than 1 million people **evacuated** the region. Highways were jammed with people leaving.

But some people stayed behind. More than 15,000 people sheltered in the Superdome stadium. Thousands more stayed home. Most were poor. They did not have a way to leave.

PEOPLE EVACUATING NEW ORLEANS

AREAS AFFECTED

A CITY FLOODS

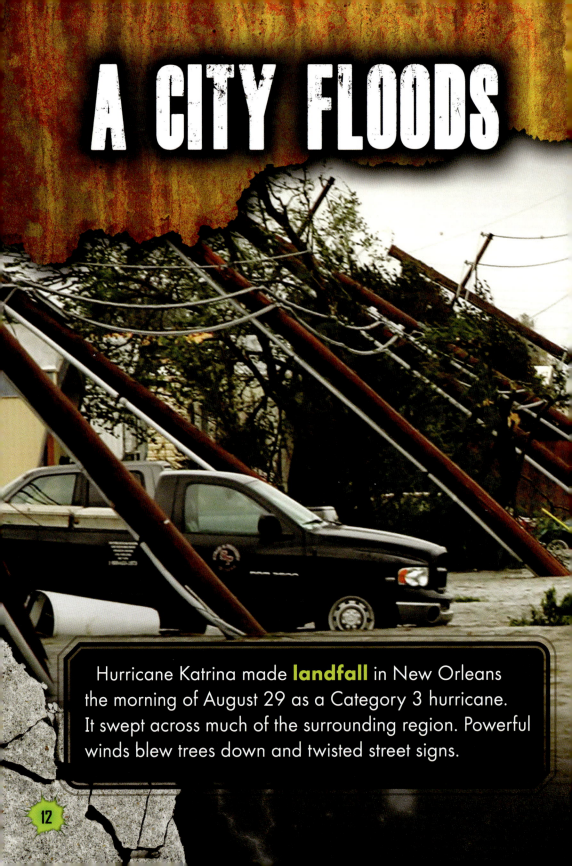

Hurricane Katrina made **landfall** in New Orleans the morning of August 29 as a Category 3 hurricane. It swept across much of the surrounding region. Powerful winds blew trees down and twisted street signs.

Katrina pushed ocean water across the land, flooding the coastline. **Storm surges** were as high as 30 feet (9 meters).

HEAVY RAIN
Around 5 to 10 inches (13 to 25 centimeters) of rain soaked the coast during the hurricane.

New Orleans used **levees** to prevent flooding. But they were old. Floodwater **seeped** through the ground under the levees. They soon failed.

FAILED LEVEE

THE STORM'S SIZE
Hurricane Katrina was 400 miles (644 kilometers) wide.

Water poured into the city. Most came from Lake Pontchartrain. Water continued to flow into the city for days. Much of New Orleans was flooded.

Floodwater filled up buildings, sometimes to the ceiling. Many people could only go to their attic or roof. Hundreds did not make it out. The **Coast Guard** rescued about 34,000 people with helicopters or boats. Some people had to wait for days to be rescued.

The floods damaged oil wells in the Gulf. More than 8 million gallons (30 million liters) of oil were spilled.

TIMELINE

AUGUST 23
The tropical depression that will become Hurricane Katrina forms over the Bahamas

AUGUST 25
The tropical depression becomes a hurricane and crosses Florida

AUGUST 28
Hurricane Katrina becomes a Category 5 hurricane over the Gulf of Mexico

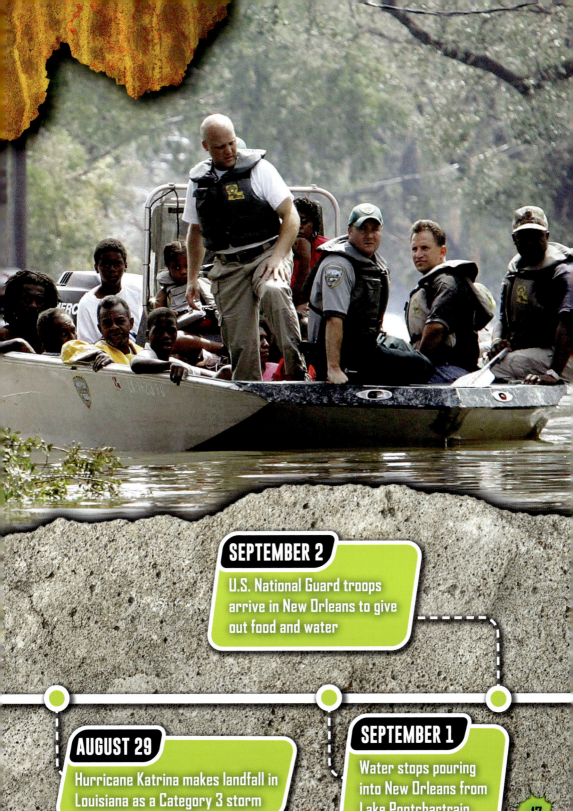

SEPTEMBER 2
U.S. National Guard troops arrive in New Orleans to give out food and water

AUGUST 29
Hurricane Katrina makes landfall in Louisiana as a Category 3 storm

SEPTEMBER 1
Water stops pouring into New Orleans from Lake Pontchartrain

17

MORE HELP ARRIVES

NATIONAL GUARD HANDING OUT SUPPLIES

18

Many survivors had no food and water. The **National Guard** arrived with supplies on September 2. The U.S. Army also searched houses for people who needed help. It took 43 days to pump the floodwater out of the city.

Katrina caused more than $160 billion in damage. It was the costliest natural disaster in U.S. history.

SLOW REBUILD

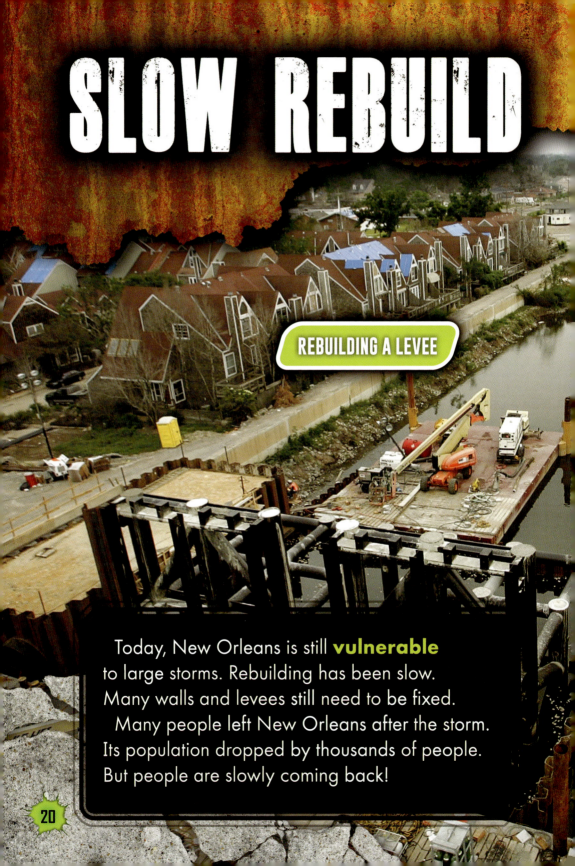

REBUILDING A LEVEE

Today, New Orleans is still **vulnerable** to large storms. Rebuilding has been slow. Many walls and levees still need to be fixed.

Many people left New Orleans after the storm. Its population dropped by thousands of people. But people are slowly coming back!

PREPARATION KIT

WATER

FOOD THAT WILL NOT SPOIL

BATTERIES

BATTERY-POWERED RADIO

GENERATOR

FUEL FOR GENERATOR

FIRST AID KIT

21

GLOSSARY

Coast Guard—a branch of the United States armed forces that protects people and enforces laws at sea

evacuated—left to avoid danger

landfall—the time when a hurricane hits land

levees—structures built up near bodies of water to prevent flooding

National Guard—an Army branch that mostly responds to emergencies within the United States; the National Guard also helps the Army overseas when needed.

seeped—flowed or leaked slowly

storm surges—events in which the ocean rises during a storm

tropical depression—a storm with maximum wind speeds of 38 miles (61 kilometers) per hour

tropical storm—a storm with maximum wind speeds of 73 miles (117 kilometers) miles per hour

vulnerable—in danger of being damaged

TO LEARN MORE

AT THE LIBRARY

Gagliardi, Sue. *Hurricane Katrina*. Lake Elmo, Minn.: Focus Readers, 2020.

Huddleston, Emma. *The New Orleans Levee Failure*. Minneapolis, Minn.: Abdo Publishing, 2020.

McGregor, Harriet. *Destroyed by a Hurricane!* Minneapolis, Minn.: Bearport Publishing, 2021.

ON THE WEB

FACTSURFER

Factsurfer.com gives you a safe, fun way to find more information.

1. Go to www.factsurfer.com

2. Enter "Hurricane Katrina" into the search box and click 🔍.

3. Select your book cover to see a list of related content.

INDEX

Abbott, Chris, 4
areas affected, 11
Bahamas, 6
Coast Guard, 16
damage, 12, 13, 14, 15, 16, 19
evacuated, 10
flooding, 8, 13, 14, 15, 16, 19
Florida, 6
formation, 6, 7, 8
Gulf of Mexico, 8, 16
Lake Pontchartrain, 15
levees, 14, 20
National Guard, 18, 19
National Weather Service, 8
New Orleans, 8, 10, 12, 14, 15, 20

oil, 16
population, 20
preparation kit, 21
rebuilding, 20
Saffir-Simpson scale, 9
size, 15
storm surges, 13
Superdome, 10
supplies, 18, 19
survivors, 19
timeline, 16–17
tropical depression, 6
tropical storm, 6
U.S. Army, 19
water, 4, 8, 13, 14, 15, 16, 19
winds, 6, 12

The images in this book are reproduced through the courtesy of: MichaelWarrenPix, cover; Martin Battilana Photography/ Alamy Stock Photo, CIP; Helifilms Australia/ Contributor/ Getty Images, pp. 4-5; Planet Observer/ Alamy Stock Photo, pp. 6-7; JACOPIN/ BSIP/ Alamy Stock Photo, p. 7 (hurricane graphic); FEMA/ Alamy Stock Photo, pp. 8-9; udaix, p. 9; REUTERS PHOTOGRAPHER/ Alamy Stock Photo, pp. 10-11, 12-13, 18-19; PSboom, p. 11 (United States); Jim Reed, p. 13; BOB MCMILLAN, pp. 14-15; Mario Tama/ Staff/ Getty Images, pp. 16-17, 20-21; Tarasyuk Igor, p. 21 (water); AlenKadr, p. 21 (food); robertlamphoto, p. 21 (batteries); digitalreflections, p. 21 (radio); MAXSHOT.PL, p. 21 (generator); Kitsch Bain, p. 21 (fuel); Pixel-Shot, p. 21 (first aid).